REMEMBERING YOUR FIRST LOVE:
Rekindling Your Spiritual Passion

Akinbowale Isaac Adewumi

Copyright © 2024 Akinbowale Isaac Adewumi

REMEMBERING YOUR FIRST LOVE: REKINDLING YOUR SPIRITUAL PASSION

ISBN: 978-1-989746-18-9

All rights reserved

No part of this publication may be reproduced, stored in a retrieval system or transmitted in any form or by any means, electronic, mechanical, photocopying, recording or otherwise, without prior written permission of the copyright owner.

Unless otherwise indicated, Scripture quotations are taken from the HOLY BIBLE, King James Version (KJV)

Formatting and Editing:
Taiwo Solomon Adeodu: +2348108673939

Dedication

"If ye love me, keep my commandments" (John 14:15).

Dedicated to those who love the Lord.

Table of Contents

Frontispiece — 1

Dedication — 3

Prologue — 5

1. Understanding the Love of God — 11
2. Rediscovering Your First Love — 23
3. The Power of First Love — 32
4. Nurturing Your Relationship with God — 43
5. Overcoming Obstacles to Your First Love — 57
6. The Blessings of Recalling Your First Love — 73

Epilogue — 91

Bibliography — 101

Prologue

Revelation 2:1-7 presents Jesus' message to the church in Ephesus, marking the commencement of seven exhortations to different churches within the Roman Empire. Ephesus posed distinctive challenges for followers of Christ due to its association with the emperor's cult and the worship of the Greek goddess Artemis (Acts 19:23-40). Despite these influences, the believers in Ephesus demonstrated remarkable discernment in identifying false teachings and heresies. Christ commended them for this discernment, yet He reproached them for having forsaken their "first love."

The initial fervour that characterized the Ephesians stemmed from the zeal and passion with which they embraced their salvation. They came to realize that their love for Christ was a response to His unconditional love for them, as expressed in 1 John 4:19. They understood that it was through His love that they were "made alive together with Christ" (Ephesians 2:1-5).

This revelation of their former state, dead in sin and their newfound life in Christ overwhelmed them with joy, leading to the manifestation of that joy in their lives. By reason of the immense love God bestowed upon them, the Ephesians were transformed and became vibrant in their devotion to Christ.

Their gratitude overflowed in passionate love for the Saviour, which extended, not only to one another, but also to those within their society, despite its moral corruption.

This preface sheds light on why many churches today experience decline - a portrayal, not only of a collective body, but also of individual Christians who, somewhere along their journey, allowed what is merely good to overshadow what is truly best in their spiritual lives. While this may not be the current state of our church, we must remain vigilant. Both collectively and individually, we must guard against losing our fervour, ensuring we do not emulate the condition of the church in Ephesus. That is why our text has been preserved in God's Word. It serves as a prophetic, preventive and prescriptive reminder. God desires to steer us away from resembling Ephesus.

When someone accepts Christ as their Saviour, they experience the profound joy of their "first love" for the Lord. It is a moment when God's Spirit resonates with theirs, affirming their newfound status as a child of God "The Spirit itself beareth witness with our spirit, that we are the children of God" (Romans 8:16). This initial connection brings immense wonder, joy and a sense of liberation.

Like any relationship, maintaining this connection takes effort. Just as human relationships can grow distant when neglected, so too can a believer's love for the Lord wane if not nurtured. When one fails to prioritize their relationship with God, their fervour can cool over time and their zeal for worship and service can dwindle and eventually die out.

In a vision to the Apostle John, Jesus expressed disappointment with the church in Ephesus for this very reason: "I have somewhat against thee, because thou hast left thy first love. Remember therefore from whence thou art fallen, and repent, and do the first works" (Revelation 2:4–5).

Jesus did not only identify their misstep, but also urged them to recollect the fervour of their initial bond and take action to restore it. Have you ever found yourself in this position, having drifted from the intimacy of God and needing to reignite your love for Him? Do you yearn for the warmth and closeness of your initial communion with God, but unsure of how to return to it?

Our love for the Lord can diminish for various reasons and one of them is losing sight of our dependence on Him. Initially, our acknowledgment of our need for God led us to seek salvation in Him. However, as time passes and God continues to provide for our needs, we may begin to overlook our reliance on Him. We might become self-sufficient, erroneously attributing our blessings to our own wisdom and efforts.

The church in Laodicea faced a similar challenge in their relationship with the Lord. Jesus addressed this issue directly, saying, "Thou sayest, I am rich, and increased with goods, and have need of nothing; and knowest not that thou art wretched, and miserable, and poor, and blind, and naked" (Revelation 3:17). Their complacency and self-reliance blinded them to their true spiritual state.

This pattern of forgetting our need for God is not new; it recurs throughout Scripture and remains relevant in our lives today. Recognizing and admitting our ongoing need for God's provision, guidance and grace is essential for maintaining a vibrant and flourishing relationship with Him.

Jesus provided clear guidance to the Ephesian church on how to restore their first love: "Yet I hold this against you: You have forsaken the love you had at first. Consider how far you have fallen! Repent and do the things you did at first. If you do not repent, I will come to you and remove your lampstand from its place" (Revelation 2:4–5 NIV, emphasis added).

Reflecting on your initial encounter with Christ and the love you felt for Him can serve as a starting point to discern any shifts in your relationship with God over time. Ask yourself whether your sense of need for God has grown stronger or weaker since your salvation experience.

Are you less fervent and engaged in spiritual matters now than you once were? If so, the first step in reigniting your first love is to repent of your apathy towards God.

Repentance entails a change of mind, heart and direction. Turn away from the thoughts, attitudes and behaviours that have diverted your focus from wholehearted devotion to the Lord.

This principle is so pivotal that Jesus emphasized it twice. Repent, accept God's forgiveness and realign yourself with His purposes for your life. After recalling and repenting, reaffirm your commitment to engage in the foundational activities of your faith.

Essentially, revisit the practices and disciplines you eagerly embraced when you first encountered the Lord and desired to deepen your relationship with Him. These initial works often involve fundamental spiritual disciplines such as prayer, studying the Scriptures, meditation, generosity, fasting and serving.

As we mature in our understanding of the Bible and God's expectations for His followers, we may become preoccupied with various "good works" aimed at enhancing our relationships with others. Unfortunately, this can lead us to overlook the essential spiritual disciplines intended to fortify our most crucial relationship, our relationship with God. The term "works" implies exertion is necessary.

Rekindling your first love demands effort on your part, yet God graciously empowers you to follow through. These initial works, including the disciplines of the Christian life, once brought you joy when you first tasted salvation. However, they can lose their freshness or priority if neglected. Recall the joy that filled your spirit in those early days. Each of these practices is intricately woven into God's design to deepen your intimate communion with Him.

CHAPTER ONE

UNDERSTANDING THE LOVE OF GOD

Introduction

The initial love we have for Jesus springs forth when we are granted a glimpse of His divine beauty and worth, stirring within us a holy longing that cannot be appeased by anything other than God Himself. These new, sanctified desires, birthed by the Spirit of God, take hold of us, causing us to yearn and ache for more of Him until our longing is met with His abundance. These yearnings are not passive; they profoundly impact the direction of our lives, redirecting our affections to their core.

Drawing from biblical teachings, "remembering your first love" often refers to the fervent devotion and passion that believers initially experience when they come to faith. It is a call to maintain that intensity of love and commitment to God, despite the distractions and challenges of life. This concept is notably mentioned in Revelation 2:1-7, where the church in Ephesus is commended for their deeds and perseverance, but admonished for forsaking their first love. Here is a reflective piece inspired by this theme:

In the quiet of the morning, before the world awakes,
We recall the fiery passion, the first love that shakes
The very core of our being, with a divine embrace,
A love so pure and zealous, it's a never-ending chase.

Remember, O my soul, the heights from which you've fallen,
The first whispers of truth, that your heart did embolden.
Return to the sacred fervour, the joy of salvation's call,
For the greatest love of all, should never fade or pall.

It's the love that first moved us, to kneel at mercy's seat,
Where grace was freely given, and our Saviour did we meet.
Let not routine or complacency, steal what was once ablaze,
But fan the flames of first love, and live in its warm rays.

For the love of Christ compels us, to seek His face anew,
To serve with the same ardor, as when faith was fresh and true.
May we never forget our first love, nor the path that we have trod,
For the heart of our devotion, is the living God.

This piece reflects on the importance of sustaining our initial love and enthusiasm for God, as well as the spiritual journey of returning to that foundational affection when we find ourselves distant. It is a reminder to cherish and prioritize our relationship with God, which is the essence of our faith.

When Jesus beckons us, as He did to the church in Ephesus, to return to our first love for Him, He calls us back to that initial thirst and longing for Him, to rekindle that desire once more. He reminds us that the deep ache we experienced for Him at the beginning was not of our own creation, but His divine intervention upon us. He has not forgotten or deviated from His purpose to answer and fulfill the longing He has placed within us. When He desires to draw us closer to Himself, He stirs that ache within us, prompting us to pursue Him once more.

Fervent, holy desires are inseparable from our love for Jesus. They are integral components of our initial love for Him and are never meant to be abandoned or diminished. These desires are intertwined with the ultimate love the Lord is cultivating within us, destined to mature and intensify over time. Love and longing are intricately linked; to separate them is to lose the essence of both. True love for Jesus necessitates a longing for Him and genuine desire springs forth from love.

Therefore, to love Jesus is to yearn for Him. Longing and desire are the pointed aspects of love, driving us to endure the pain of delay and the ache of unsatisfied longing, steadfast in our conviction that Jesus alone is the source of all satisfaction. Our longing for Jesus testifies to both His beauty and our anticipation of the glorious day when our faith will become sight and our hope will be fully realized.

Loving Jesus in this manner isn't always easy, but a love devoid of longing is not genuine love. The initial sweetness of longing for Jesus often gives way to greater challenges as the years pass and we encounter setbacks in our lives. When delays and confusion arise, we may be tempted to shield our hearts from the vulnerability of our initial yearnings for God.

The trials and obstacles we face may seem like God's rejection when we fail to grasp the sacred origins of our hunger and His zealous desire to fulfill it. These awakened desires, stirred by God's hand, are pivotal to our glorious future, marking the starting point toward our ultimate destination.

What we often overlook and what my own heart needed a shift in perspective on, is that the delays we encounter are not refusals to our prayers by God. Instead, they serve as preparatory steps to ready us for the fulfillment of our longing to know Him intimately and walk in fellowship with Him. Though there may be pain in the longing, He calls us to embrace this vulnerable yearning as an expression of our love for Him. He urges us to persevere through the delays we face, remaining steadfast in our belief, desire and longing for His fullness with hearts wide open.

Recently, memories from many decades ago resurfaced within me upon encountering a parallel of Ron Highfield's insight and Kevin Owen's article on "Rekindling Your Spiritual Passion." This piece emphasizes the significance for Christians to recollect and cherish memories of their initial love for God, the moments when we were deeply impacted by relationships, mentors, literature, causes and purposes that moulded us and left a lasting imprint on our lives. In this reflection, I aim to join in celebrating these pivotal chapters of our spiritual journeys.

The Perfect Love of God

The perfect love of God is a love that surpasses all understanding and human comprehension. It is a love that is unconditional, unchanging, and unwavering. This love is demonstrated through the sacrifice of Jesus Christ on the cross for the forgiveness of our sins. God's perfect love is a love that is pure, holy and righteous. It is a love that is not based on our actions or merit, but solely on God's grace and mercy. This love is constant and never fails, even when we fail Him.

God's perfect love is a love that is transformative and life-changing. It has the power to heal, restore and redeem us from our brokenness and sin. It is a love that brings hope, peace and joy to our lives. As believers, we are called to walk in the perfect love of God and to share this love with others. By doing so, we reflect the character of God and fulfill His greatest commandments to love Him and love our neighbours as ourselves.

The perfect love of God is a profound and central theme in Christian theology, embodying the nature of God's relationship with humanity. This concept is deeply rooted in Scripture and reflects the core of God's character, His actions throughout redemptive history, and His invitation to believers to live in and through His love. The perfect love of God is encapsulated in 1 John 4:16, which declares, "God is love. Whoever lives in love lives in God, and God in them." This verse highlights that love is not merely an attribute of God, but His very essence. To comprehend the perfect love of God, we must look at various dimensions of His love as revealed in the Bible.

Unconditional and Sacrificial Love

God's love is unconditional as it is given without regard to merit or worthiness. Romans 5:8 states, "But God demonstrates his own love for us in this: While we were still sinners, Christ died for us" (NIV). This demonstrates that God's love is not based on our actions but on His gracious character. The sacrificial nature of God's love is most vividly expressed in the sending of His Son, Jesus Christ, to die for humanity's sins. John 3:16, perhaps the most well-known verse, affirms, "For God so loved the world that he gave his one and only Son, that whoever believes in him shall not perish, but have eternal life." (NIV).

Redeeming and Transforming Love

The perfect love of God is also redemptive and transforming. It seeks to redeem humanity from the bondage of sin and transform lives to reflect His holiness. Ephesians 2:4-5 emphasizes this: "But because of his great love for us, God, who is rich in mercy, made us alive with Christ even when we were dead in transgressions — it is by grace you have been saved." (NIV). This passage highlights that God's love brings life and transformation to those who accept it, moving them from spiritual death to life in Christ.

Faithful and Everlasting Love

Another aspect of God's perfect love is its faithfulness and eternal nature. Lamentations 3:22-23 reassures us, "Because of the Lord's great love we are not consumed, for his compassions never fail. They are new every morning; great is your faithfulness." (NIV). God's love endures forever, and His promises are reliable. This enduring love offers believers a foundation of trust and hope, knowing that God's love will never waver or diminish.

Perfect Love Casts Out Fear

The apostle John also teaches that perfect love drives out fear. In 1 John 4:18, it is written, "There is no fear in love. But perfect love drives out fear, because fear has to do with punishment. The one who fears is not made perfect in love" (NIV). This verse speaks to the security found in God's love. Believers do not need to fear judgment or condemnation because God's love, fully realized through Jesus Christ, brings peace and assurance of salvation.

Love as the Foundation of Relationships

Jesus emphasized that love should be the foundation of all relationships. When asked about the greatest commandment, He responded, "Love the Lord your God with all your heart and with all your soul and with all your mind. This is the first and greatest commandment. And the second is like it: Love your neighbor as yourself." (Matthew 22:37-39 NIV). This teaching underscores that living in God's perfect love involves loving others selflessly and sacrificially, thus reflecting God's own love for us.

Therefore, understanding the perfect love of God towards humanity calls believers to reflect deeply on the nature of God's love—its unconditional, sacrificial, redeeming, faithful and fear-dispelling aspects. This love is the cornerstone of Christian faith and life, urging believers to live in such a way that God's love is evident in their relationships and actions. Embracing this love transforms individuals and communities positively, drawing them closer to the fullness of life that God intends for His creation.

In other words, the perfect love of God is a gift beyond measure that we can never earn or deserve by our works. It is a love that is eternal and everlasting; it is the foundation of our faith and salvation. This explanation provides a comprehensive view of "The perfect love of God," encouraging believers to explore and embody this divine love in their daily lives. May we always be mindful of God's perfect love and strive to live in the light of His love each and every day.

The Importance of Remembering Your First Love

In the admonition to the church in Ephesus, the Apostle John references the time when you first grasped the unfathomable love of the Creator of the heavens and the earth. It was a moment filled with awe and reverence, as everything seemed new and transformed, including your perception of yourself as someone worthy of salvation and guidance by the Lord of lords. Undoubtedly, there may have been resistance to the revelation that Christ esteemed you valuable and entrusted you to share His love with those in your church community, as you united in singing His praises.

The early church in Ephesus was renowned for several noteworthy attributes. They were known for their diligence in good works, their unwavering support for the truth and their resolute stance against false teachings. These characteristics were emblematic of a community deeply committed to living out the teachings of Christ and upholding the purity of the Gospel message.

In the Book of Revelation, the Apostle John delivers a sobering message to a church, stating, "Remember therefore from whence thou art fallen" (Revelation 2:5). This warning underscores the peril of losing one's spiritual fervour for the Lord and His Kingdom's work.

When a believer embarks on their journey with Christ, they often experience a profound sense of gratitude, wonder and awe at Jesus' love for them and the value He places upon their lives. Initially, this newfound faith may overflow with joy and a fervent desire to share the good news with others. However, as the believer progresses in their walk, serves and matures in the faith, this spiritual vitality can be inadvertently replaced, displaced or even distorted by a sense of pride or pretence.

At some juncture in the Christian journey, one may come to the realization that the passion they once felt for Christ has diminished, along with their fervour for sharing the gospel with others. This serves as a timely reminder to regularly assess the state of our spiritual fervency and to guard against any complacency or distractions that may hinder our intimacy with the Lord and our zeal for His Kingdom's work.

Neglecting Your First Love Affects Your Spiritual Life

Many believers encounter a struggle with waning spiritual passion. Though they may remain engaged in church activities, the fervour and excitement that characterized their early Christian journey have dwindled. Instead, they find themselves caught in a state of lethargy and indifference, merely going through the motions without genuine zeal. Their condition is not typically marked by hostility or opposition; rather, they are spiritually dormant, stagnant or evading the vibrant testimony of Jesus Christ.

Despite maintaining a semblance of Christian practice, they have lost the enthusiasm and vitality that once defined their faith. What was once a fervent love and devotion has been replaced by apathy and mechanical service. The initial fire has dimmed, leaving behind a sense of monotony and mediocrity. This serves as a reminder to continually assess the state of our spiritual fervency and to guard against complacency and spiritual stagnation. It calls for a rekindling of the flame of devotion and a renewed commitment to wholehearted service to the Lord.

In our journey through life, we often find ourselves engaged in various activities, pursuits or causes. Initially, our involvement is fueled by passion and enthusiasm. However, over time, that passion can wane and we may find ourselves merely going through the motions, giving these endeavours just enough attention to appease others and quiet our own conscience. What once brought us joy and fulfillment become routine and before we realize it, we are consumed by criticism, hate, resentment, disillusionment and apathy.

It is worth noting that no one embarks on a journey of faith, seeks after God, undergoes baptism or joins a church, small group or ministry with the intention of embracing drudgery and legalism. Yet, we' have all witnessed individuals who initially displayed fervent passion and dedication gradually lose their enthusiasm and zeal. Consequently, they lose interest, influence, joy, effectiveness and satisfaction in their endeavours. Some may even choose to walk away altogether.

This serves as a sobering reminder to continually evaluate the state of our heart and motivations in all that we do. It prompts us to guard against complacency and spiritual indifference and to actively seek renewal and revitalization in our pursuits, ensuring that our actions are driven by genuine passion and devotion rather than mere obligation or habit.

CHAPTER TWO

REDISCOVERING YOUR FIRST LOVE

In the book of Revelation, Jesus commends the church in Ephesus for their perseverance and hard work, but He also rebukes them for forsaking their first love. "Nevertheless, I have somewhat against thee, because thou hast left thy first love (Revelation 2:4). This serves as a powerful reminder to all believers to constantly evaluate our relationship with God and ensure that our love for Him remains fervent and passionate.

When we first come to faith in Christ, the love and excitement we feel can be overwhelming. We are eager to spend time in His presence, to study His Word and to share His love with others. However, as time goes by and the busyness of life takes over, we can easily lose sight of that initial love and enthusiasm. So, how do we rediscover our first love for God? The answer lies in returning to the basics of our faith. We must prioritize spending time in prayer, reading the Bible and worshiping with other believers. We must seek to cultivate a deeper relationship with God and allow Him to renew our hearts and minds.

Additionally, we must guard against allowing the things of this world to distract us from our love for God. Material possessions, relationships and even good works can all become idols if we allow them to take precedence over our relationship with Him. We must constantly examine our hearts and ask God to reveal any areas where we have allowed our love for Him to grow cold.

Reflecting on our first love involves recalling the profound sacrifice of Good Friday, where God's sacrificial death for our sins is symbolized. The love demonstrated through the cross surpasses all other loves, even if our initial response may have contained elements of infatuation. Though we may believe we've walked this path before and know what must be done, the need to revisit this experience suggests that we did not fully comprehend or appreciate its significance initially.

This is a common occurrence in our spiritual lives, akin to the Ephesian church's initial love that later lacked depth. In such moments, our natural response should be to move beyond superficial emotions and cultivate a deeper, more profound love that arises from truly knowing and understanding the object of our affection.

Naturally, one might question, "How does one repent of losing their first love?" or "What steps should one take to regain it?" This leads us to a crucial insight. While it may appear unconventional, God directs us to remember the fervent love we experienced during the early stages of romantic relationships.

Recall those moments when thoughts of your beloved consumed your mind and heart beyond mere infatuation. These deep feelings of affection and devotion epitomize the love that may have been displaced by other affections. God simply commands us to revisit our initial love and then repent.

In the case of the Ephesian believers, their primary love for God had been supplanted by a love for their church community. Similarly, in our lives, our devotion to God may have been overshadowed by other emotional attachments. The solution lies in rejecting selfish emotionalism and recalling our first love for God. As we do so, that love will naturally be reignited within us, restoring our fervent devotion and intimacy with Him.

Ultimately, rediscovering our first love for God requires intentionality and commitment. It requires us to daily surrender our lives to Him, to seek His will above all else and to allow His love to overflow in us and through us to those around us. May we never forget the depth of His love for us and may we continually strive to love Him with all of our heart, soul, mind and strength.

Reflecting on Your Initial Encounter with God

Reflecting on your initial encounter with God serves as a powerful reminder of your first love for Him. During that time, you were deeply and passionately devoted to God, consumed by a fervent love for Him. This introspection should prompt you to assess your current relationship with God, whether your passion for Him remains as intense or if it has diminished over time. This self-awareness can stir a longing within you to rekindle the love you once had, motivating you to pursue the restoration of your fervour for God. Your passion for God originally stemmed from the love you harboured for Him.

To reignite that passion, it is crucial to revisit your initial encounter with God and recognize the work He was doing in your life during that period. By recalling these pivotal moments, you become more attuned to the spiritual fervency that enabled you to experience such encounters with God. This awareness serves as a catalyst for reigniting your passion for Him, propelling you towards the goal of recapturing the depth of your love for God.

Upon pondering your initial encounter with God, you will gain insight into areas of your life where your passion for Him has diminished. This revelation will unveil the essence of your first love. During that time, you were fervent about engaging with God's Word, prayer, evangelism, serving others, worship and various activities that reflected your love for Him.

After revisiting your initial encounter and identifying the manifestations of your love for God, take a moment to examine your present lifestyle. Consider how you interact with God, your priorities and the activities that occupy your time and attention. Have you neglected God's Word and prayer in favour of other pursuits?

Have you ceased sharing your faith and serving fellow believers? Do you approach worship services with indifference, selecting only those activities within the church that align with your preferences?

This introspection allows you to discern any deviations from your initial fervour and identify areas where your love for God may have waned. It serves as an opportunity for repentance and realignment with God's priorities, prompting you to recommit to a lifestyle characterized by wholehearted devotion and passionate pursuit of Him.

Recalling the Joy and Zeal of Your Early Faith

These experiences are not unique to me; they have echoed through countless ages past and will continue to resonate in countless ages to come. The annals of church history bear witness to the illumination they have brought. No believer, regardless of their stature or strength, is exempt from such encounters. Do you remember the early days of your faith? Can you recollect the profound intimacy when you first fell in love with Jesus?

As a new believer, my passion for Christ was so intense that meditating on the cross would captivate me for hours. I would be overcome with uncontrollable weeping, tears flowing in torrents of profound emotion. I could not bear to be apart from Him; my love for Him consumed me entirely. Neglecting even the basic necessities of food and water, I grew thin with the fervour of my devotion. Every moment was devoted to Him and loving Him became the central theme of my life. I was consumed with thoughts of Him and my heart yearned to be in His presence continually.

Together, we immersed ourselves in Scripture and fervently preached the gospel. The thought of willfully sinning was abhorrent to us; we would have preferred death over such transgression. Our minds remained undistracted by lesser concerns and we were fully committed to our love for Him.

In Revelation 2:1-5, Jesus addresses the church in Ephesus. This congregation displayed outward signs of spiritual strength. They were diligent, obedient, faithful and discerning. They abhorred immorality and evil, patiently endured hardship and worked tirelessly for the sake of the gospel. They upheld sound doctrine and were vigilant in identifying false teachings. Their spiritual dedication seemed commendable, as evidenced by Jesus' acknowledgment of their deeds. However, despite their outward appearance, Jesus saw beyond the surface.

Jesus revealed a deeper truth about their condition: they had forsaken their first love. In the midst of their busyness and adherence to righteousness, they had lost the fervent passion that characterized their initial love for God. Have you found that your zeal to pursue God has veered off course? Are you stuck in a routine rather than passionately pursuing Him?

Perhaps you feel distant from the joyous fervour you once experienced in your relationship with God. Jesus empathizes with your struggle. He is compassionate and understands the condition of your heart.

Identifying the Factors that Diminish Your Passion

Identifying the root causes of the problem does not automatically free you from it. It is essential to recognize that the lack of passion is often deeply rooted in various life challenges. Overcoming these challenges is key to reigniting your spiritual fervour. This process of overcoming is what we will refer to as "the journey of rekindling passion."

Identifying and understanding the underlying causes of waning devotion should serve as a starting point, empowering you to transition to the next stage, the process of revival. This phase involves addressing and cleansing the roots of the identified problems, whether they are acknowledged or not. This marks our next step towards recovery.

We trust in God's complete and perfect plan of salvation. Even when we find ourselves on precarious ground or mired in difficulty, God extends His hand to guide us. Have the demands of daily life consumed your time and attention to the extent that you neglect the central purpose of life, to cultivate a relationship with Christ?

When you pray, do you find yourself reciting words mechanically, devoid of heartfelt emotion or do you experience the vitality of genuine fervour as you commune with God?

Prayer infused with present, sensitive and pure emotion is truly beautiful and when God touches our hearts in response to our prayers, we once again feel the fire burning within us. Do you derive a sense of satisfaction from participating in religious activities such as church services, meetings or community service only to feel empty and despondent afterwards as if the meaning of our religious lives eludes you in moments of solitude?

Do you prioritize daily prayer, Bible reading and meditation on God's Word or do you find it challenging to devote time to these spiritual disciplines? Reflecting on these questions may reveal the depth of your spiritual engagement. Merely engaging in religious activities without experiencing the true meaning behind them can diminish their quality. This is not passion; it is merely adhering to tradition, a form of superficiality devoid of genuine spiritual depth.

Given the profound significance of rekindling your first love, there are several vital steps you should take to accomplish this endeavour. First and foremost, it is crucial to identify the factors that have contributed to the waning of your passion. Self-awareness plays a pivotal role in reigniting your spiritual fervour. So, it is essential to introspectively examine the roots of the issue.

Consider asking yourself a series of probing questions to delve into where and when your passion began to diminish. Here are a few questions to guide your introspection, though you should feel free to incorporate additional inquiries pertinent to your situation so as to have a robust appraisal:

1. Have the demands of daily life overshadowed my pursuit of intimacy with Christ?

2. Do I approach prayer and spiritual disciplines with genuine fervour or have they become mere rituals?

3. Do I derive fulfillment from religious activities or do they leave me feeling empty and disconnected?

4. Am I prioritizing regular communion with God through prayer, Scripture reading and meditation?

5. Do I still live in the joy of salvation and holy lifestyle that characterized my early Christian experience?

By honestly confronting these questions and engaging in thorough introspection, you can begin to uncover the underlying causes of your diminished passion and take proactive steps towards revitalizing your spiritual life.

CHAPTER THREE

THE POWER OF FIRST LOVE

Our first experiences of love, whether positive or negative, profoundly shape our emotional development and impact our self-esteem. They teach us empathy, communication skills and resilience, guiding us as we navigate relationships and define our values. While the reasons behind the power of first love may seem elusive, it is the culmination of myriad small details that make it so significant.

First love is characterized by intense emotions and passion, often leaving an indelible mark on our hearts. It represents our initial encounter with love outside the familial realm, fostering a sense of belonging and connection unlike any other. Even after the relationship has ended, first love remains a defining aspect of our identity.

Indeed, first love holds a unique place in our hearts. It serves as a benchmark for future relationships, setting the standard for how we love and expect to be loved. Its memory can evoke feelings of nostalgia, longing and joy, reminding us of the profound impact it has had on our lives. In reflecting on Jesus' admonition to the church in Ephesus, as recorded in Revelation 3, we are confronted with the sobering reality of spiritual lukewarmness. Christ's words, "I know thy works, that thou art neither cold nor hot: I would thou wert cold or hot. So then because thou art lukewarm, and neither cold nor hot, I will spue thee out of my mouth" (Revelation 3:15-16), serve as a sad reminder of the dangers of spiritual complacency.

Consider the story of an eleventh-century missionary who left his place of assignment and was unable to complete his assigned tasks. When his former leader encountered him years later in the city, he inquired about the missionary's departure. The missionary confessed, that the work was too difficult. However, the leader offered a profound insight saying that the rule is for those who cannot do the work. Those who are engaged in the work belong to the Kingdom and that encompasses everyone within the ministry.

This narrative underscores the importance of active engagement in spiritual pursuits. Just as the missionary struggled with the demands of his calling, we too may encounter challenges and obstacles along our spiritual journey. Yet, Christ calls us to wholehearted devotion and diligent service, not to a lukewarm faith devoid of fervour and commitment. May we heed the words of our Lord and Saviour, striving to be fervent in spirit, serving the Lord with zeal and dedication. Let us not be content with spiritual mediocrity, but rather embrace the call to wholehearted discipleship, knowing that our labour in the Lord is never in vain (1 Corinthians 15:58).

Understanding the Transformative Nature of First Love

The transformative nature of first love is a concept deeply rooted in the biblical narrative and is exemplified in the relationship between God and His people. In the book of Exodus, God's unconditional love and faithfulness towards the Israelites are vividly displayed as He leads them out of slavery in Egypt and into the Promised Land. This act of redemption and deliverance is a powerful demonstration of God's first love for His chosen people.

Similarly, in the New Testament, we see Jesus Christ embodying the perfect expression of first love through His sacrificial death on the cross. The Apostle John captures this profound truth in his first epistle when he declares, "Herein is love, not that we loved God, but that he loved us, and sent his Son to be the propitiation for our sins." (1 John 4:10).

This selfless act of love not only serves as a model for us to follow, but also reveals the transformative power of first love in our lives. The transformative nature of first love requires us to acknowledge the depths of God's love for us and to respond in kind.

Just as the church in Ephesus was commended for their perseverance and hard work, but rebuked for forsaking their first love, we must constantly evaluate our relationship with God and ensure that our love for Him remains fervent and passionate.

To experience the transformative power of first love, we must cultivate a deep and intimate relationship with God through prayer, studying His Word and fellowshipping with other believers. By prioritizing our relationship with Him above all else, we allow His love to renew our hearts, minds and spirits, transforming us from the inside out.

Experiencing love for the Christ brings about a profound transformation within oneself, impacting every aspect of one's being. This transformational love shakes the very foundations of one's beliefs, challenging long-held convictions and ushering in new perspectives. It is akin to a spiritual awakening and related to the profound revelations experienced during a near-death encounter.

This transformative love compels individuals to re-evaluate their relationships, both with others and with the divine. It empowers them to embrace vulnerability, to confront past wrongs and to seek forgiveness from those they have hurt. Even if forgiveness is not granted, they find solace in knowing that they have made sincere efforts to seek reconciliation.

Moreover, this transformative love enables individuals to release the burden of anger and resentment that they may have carried from past grievances. Instead of clinging to victimhood, they choose to let go of negative emotions, recognizing that they only serve to hinder their spiritual growth.

Conversely, when others seek forgiveness from them, those imbued with transformational love extend grace and understanding, realizing the frailty of human nature and the propensity for misunderstandings and conflicts. They embrace forgiveness wholeheartedly, transcending petty grievances and choosing to focus on the deeper connection of love that binds humanity together.

In essence, transformational love grants individuals a heightened sense of empathy, compassion and forgiveness. It allows them to see beyond surface-level conflicts and grievances, fostering deeper understanding and reconciliation in relationships. As they radiate this love outward, they become beacons of healing and reconciliation in a world often plagued by discord and strife.

When one experiences the profound love of the God, it instills a deep sense of purpose and a desire to bring about positive change in the world. This transformative love compels individuals to re-evaluate their priorities and embrace their role as instruments of peace and reconciliation.

As this love takes root in the heart, there is a strong inclination to mend broken relationships and reconcile estranged family members and friends. Also, the transformative power of love seeks to dissolve barriers erected by anger and resentment, guiding individuals towards forgiveness and reconciliation.

Furthermore, transformational love prompts individuals to engage in introspection, leading to a deeper understanding of their own motivations and actions. It fosters empathy and compassion, allowing them to forgive both themselves and others for past mistakes and transgressions. While intelligence may provide insight, it is wisdom, fueled by love and experience that enables individuals to make wise choices in life.

This wisdom empowers them to navigate life's challenges with grace and discernment, choosing paths that lead to growth and fulfillment. In the end, life's most profound lessons are encapsulated in love. Love liberates individuals from the shackles of external circumstances and empowers them to find peace and serenity within themselves. It teaches them to detach from outcomes beyond their control and to find solace in the inner core of their being. In this journey of love and self-discovery, individuals find a deep sense of inner peace that remains unshaken by external turmoil. It is a peace that transcends understanding, offering comfort and assurance even in the midst of life's storms.

As transformation takes hold, it revolutionizes every aspect of your being. Some may perceive you differently while others may struggle to understand the profound changes taking place within you. Yet, as the transformation deepens, external opinions become insignificant compared to the overwhelming grace and love enveloping your life.

In this journey of transformation, you confront your inner demons and conquer them with the power of the love of God.

Mistakes and shortcomings are acknowledged as part of your human nature, but love reveals your true identity as a beloved child of the Creator. It invites you to embrace your divine essence and recognize the inherent glory and majesty within you.

Beyond this, understanding the transformative nature of first love compels us to guard against anything that may hinder or distract us from our love for God. We must be vigilant in recognizing and rooting out any idols or worldly desires that threaten to diminish our love for Him.

Moreover, transformative love leads you on a quest for truth and self-discovery, guiding you to the source of all love and creativity, the Almighty God. As you delve deeper into this quest, you come to understand the profound connection between your existence and the divine love that sustains all of creation.

Recognizing the Impact of First Love on Your Relationship with God

As beloved children of God, we often anticipate His compassion and understanding towards our joys and struggles. Yet, have we considered God's own joys and sorrows? Is our relationship with Him one that fosters empathy for His experiences? God yearns for a mutual friendship, a love relationship characterized by reciprocity, where we freely give of ourselves to nurture gratitude and intimacy. This transcends any relationship built on guilt, obligation or coercion. It is a bond of liberation, expanding beyond ourselves and allowing God's blessings to flow through us to others. For we are all cherished by Him. We cannot truly love God out of obligation or guilt as such constraints stifle freedom. Instead, let us embrace the freedom of genuine love, a love that springs from gratitude and moves us to share His love with others, enriching our relationship with Him and fostering deeper intimacy.

As believers, if we neglect to grasp the significance of our first love for Christ, we miss out on cultivating a profound passion for Him. Consequently, we may find ourselves merely going through the motions of faith rather than truly living by it. However, if we earnestly pursue our initial love for Christ, our hearts will be filled with the power and guidance of the Holy Spirit. This divine empowerment enables us to boldly proclaim the Gospel, declare Jesus as Lord and offer Him sincere praise and adoration. Our love for Him ignites a flame within us that cannot be extinguished, compelling us to speak out and share His love with others.

Reflect on when you first encountered Christ, your heart overflowed with love for Him and He consumed your thoughts. Every aspect of your life revolved around Him and you eagerly shared His message with others. Recapturing this fervent love is paramount for every believer. It is this initial passion that propelled us into our journey of faith. There is nothing more vital than experiencing the revival of love that consumes and transforms us anew.

Embracing the Renewal and Restoration of Your First Love

Consider where you most need renewal in your life. How deeply do you long for God's mercies to permeate your circumstances? Know that God has a divine plan, to teach, guide and lead you into a profound encounter with Him that will refresh your spirit with His boundless goodness and love. Spending intimate time alone with God holds tremendous value in our spiritual journey. It is in these moments that we are rejuvenated by His word and His presence, receiving daily renewal for our souls. By prioritizing God at the outset of each day, He faithfully equips us for whatever challenges lie ahead. As Scripture assures us, "The steadfast love of the Lord never ceases; his mercies never come to an end; they are new every morning; great is your faithfulness" (Lamentations 3:22-23).

Create space in your day to meet with God, allowing yourself to experience the gentle rain of His presence that restores and revives the dry and weary places within your heart. Each individual may offer a different perspective and it is important to honour and respect each viewpoint. Some may have known from the outset that they would depart at the first opportunity while others may have determined to postpone their return until a later time. If you have sought guidance on how to reignite your first love, even if you harbour some degree of uncertainty, as many of us do, it signifies that you are genuinely attuned to God's voice and earnestly seek His plan for restoration.

In this process, we come to realize that we may not have cherished our church community as deeply as we ought to have done. We failed to fully appreciate the freedom and favour bestowed upon us, a privilege not afforded to everyone. To rekindle our fervour for God and to reunite our hearts and spirits as a church, it is essential not merely to open the doors, but to persistently seek Him, continually knocking at the door of His presence.

As we earnestly pursue God, both within the confines of our church walls and beyond, we witness miracles unfolding in our midst. We trust that God is preparing something greater for a larger assembly. If He has yet to signal that it is time to move forward, then let us embrace the journey from wherever we find ourselves presently.

We are in the process of rebuilding, diligently striving to maintain Jesus as our foremost Love. We are persistently seeking, knocking on every door and petitioning the Holy Spirit, "We crave more of You. We desperately need more." I wholeheartedly empathize with this sentiment. However, may I encourage you to pursue God with unwavering dedication, regardless of your physical location?

Even if it means remaining at home longer than others, who is to say that you cannot experience profound encounters with Jesus in the intimacy of your living room? Quality time spent with Him in the solitude of your home may far surpass the distractions that sometimes accompany gatherings at church.

If rushing back into communal worship prematurely threatens to yield only decreasing changes in our spiritual climate, then let us collectively agree to exercise patience. Let us choose to prioritize depth over haste, trusting that God's timing is perfect and that He is orchestrating a profound transformation in our midst in our journey back to our first love.

CHAPTER FOUR

NURTURING YOUR RELATIONSHIP WITH GOD

When we surrender our lives to Christ, the barriers separating us from God are dismantled and He takes up residence within us through His Holy Spirit. We enter into a profound relationship with the Creator of the universe, we know Him intimately and He knows us intimately. Yet, like any relationship, our connection with God requires nurturing and cultivation.

If neglected, it can grow cold and we may perceive God as distant. This distancing can lead us astray, diverting us toward destructive paths. As the Bible admonishes, "Love not the world, neither the things that are in the world. If any man love the world, the love of the Father is not in him. For all that is in the world, the lust of the flesh, and the lust of the eyes, and the pride of life, is not of the Father, but is of the world. And the world passeth away, and the lust thereof: but he that doeth the will of God abideth for ever." (1 John 2:15,17).

How do we foster a daily walk with God? Consider the dynamics of a human friendship: How do we deepen our bond with someone on a human level?

Primarily, it is through spending time together, conversing, listening, sharing concerns and offering assistance when needed. The same principle applies to our relationship with God. When we engage with His Word, the Bible, He communicates with us. Through prayer, we communicate with Him. By worshiping and obeying Him, we align ourselves with His will and participate in His divine work. Communication serves as the cornerstone of any relationship. Devoting one-on-one time to converse with God is indispensable. It is an opportunity to present our needs, seek guidance and express gratitude. Prayer emerges as the simplest and most accessible means of nurturing our relationship with Christ.

Dedicating time to study the Word beyond Sunday service is essential. Thanks to digital media and technology, we now have easy access to the Scriptures through various Bible apps. Make the most of these resources. Additionally, participate in church Bible studies to enrich your understanding with midweek lessons. After engaging with the Word, take time to reflect on its significance. How does it resonate with you? How does it apply to the circumstances you are facing? Reflecting on His goodness in your life and on the narratives of faith within Christianity contributes to the deepening of your relationship with God. As Psalms 150:6 exhorts, "Let every thing that hath breath praise the Lord."

Praising Jesus, Who is merciful and faithful, is a potent expression of gratitude. Therefore, expressing thankfulness is a crucial aspect of connecting with Him.

Personal worship serves as an act of surrender and release. Through worship, you open yourself to God's presence and allow Him to speak into your life. Remember, worship is not merely an external display; it must also spring from the depths of our spirit. Taking the time to study the Word outside of Sunday service is imperative. Digital media and technology have enabled us to have The Word at our finger tips. Make use of Bible apps. In addition, go to church Bible studies to get that midweek lesson.

After studying the Word, reflect on it. What does it mean to you? How is it relevant and relatable to the situations in your life? Reflecting on all that is good in your life and on the Christian stories certainly aid in fostering your relationship. "Let every thing that hath breath praise the Lord. Praise ye the Lord" (Psalms 150:6). Jesus is merciful and faithful and praising Him is a powerful form of gratitude.

Therefore, being thankful and expressing it is vital part in connecting with Him. Our personal worship is a form of release and absolute surrender. You are opening yourself up to allow God to speak to you and come into your life. "Worship is spiritual. Our worship must be more than just an outward expression, it must also take place in our spirits" (Franklin Graham).

Cultivating a Daily Devotional Life

Daily devotion is essential for balancing our lives, allowing us to serve others while deepening our relationship with God. However, for some, challenges such as a lack of understanding, focus or inner peace during devotional reading can hinder this practice. It is important to remember that the Bible, at its core, is a book. Just as our favourite stories and narratives come alive through imagery and interpretation, so too does Scripture.

Scholars may debate the meaning and interpretation of texts, but we must always recognize that we are engaging with the words of a sovereign Spirit. Approaching the Bible with humility and openness, like children listening to a teacher or a parent telling a story, is key. We should read God's Word repeatedly, finding joy in its message and discovering wisdom in detail which we may have previously overlooked. By immersing ourselves in Scripture in this way, we can nurture a deeper connection with God and find fulfillment in our daily devotionals.

Scripture encourages us to meditate on God's Word day and night. "This book of the law shall not depart out of thy mouth; but thou shalt meditate therein day and night, that thou mayest observe to do according to all that is written therein: for then thou shalt make thy way prosperous, and then thou shalt have good success" (Joshua 1:8).

This highlights its importance in our spiritual growth. Through meditation, we can experience profound effects on both our minds and bodies. It has been scientifically proven to reduce stress and anxiety, improve focus, strengthen our immune systems and promote better sleep. Moreover, meditation fosters self-awareness and deepens our understanding of our thoughts, emotions and inner experiences. By quieting our minds and opening our hearts to God, we can develop greater compassion and empathy for ourselves and others, aligning more closely with the love and grace of Christ.

Incorporating meditation into our daily routine can enrich our spiritual life, helping us to draw closer to God and experience His presence in a profound way. Remembering your first love is central to Christian spirituality, an essential aspect of our relationship with God. In the journey of faith, two key conversations consistently arise between God and His earnest followers: discussions about prayer and engagement with Scripture. These dialogues reflect God's desire to guide His children in deepening their connection with Him.

Sadly, many believers encounter challenges in these areas. Questions like, "How do I pray when I lack the words?" or "How do I comprehend Scripture's message?" often trouble us. However, some Christians have found a rhythm in communicating with God and immersing themselves in His Word. Yet, even for them, the question persists: "How can I cultivate spiritual discipline amidst life's pressing demands?" In addressing these concerns, we recognize the importance of nurturing our relationship with God through prayer and Scripture.

Prayer is our direct line of communication with the Creator while Scripture serves as His revealed word, guiding and shaping our lives. Developing spiritual discipline involves setting aside intentional time for prayer and Bible study, even amid life's busyness. By prioritizing these spiritual practices, we create space for God to work in our hearts and lives. Through consistent prayer and immersion in Scripture, we can rediscover the fervent love we first had for God and deepen our spiritual walk with Him.

Seeking Intimacy through Prayer and Worship

Seeking intimacy with God through prayer and worship is a fundamental aspect of the Christian faith. Throughout the Bible, we are encouraged to draw near to God with sincerity and devotion, knowing that He eagerly desires to commune with us. Prayer, as taught by Jesus, is not just a religious duty, but a means of establishing a personal relationship with God. In Matthew 6:6, Jesus encourages us to pray in secret, emphasizing the intimacy of our connection with God. Prayer is our direct line of communication with the Creator of the universe, allowing us to pour out our hearts, express our deepest desires and seek guidance and strength from Him.

Worship, on the other hand, is the expression of our reverence, adoration and love for God. It involves not only singing songs of praise, but also bowing our hearts before Him in humility and awe. Psalms 95:6-7 urges us, "Come, let us bow down in worship, let us kneel before the Lord our Maker; for he is our God and we are the people of his pasture, the flock under his care." Worship is a transformative experience where we encounter the presence of God and are drawn closer to Him.

Through prayer and worship, we enter into the sacred space of God's presence where His love and grace envelop us. It is in these moments of intimacy that we find solace, strength and guidance for our lives. Just as a child seeks comfort and security in the arms of a loving parent, so too do we find refuge in the embrace of our Heavenly Father through prayer and worship.

Practical Application

Set aside dedicated time for prayer and worship: Schedule regular times throughout your day or week to spend in prayer and worship, whether it is in the morning, during lunch breaks or in the evening before bed.

Create a Sacred Space: Find a quiet and comfortable place where you can pray and worship without distractions. This could be a corner of your room, a garden or a peaceful outdoor setting.

Use Scripture as a Guide: Draw inspiration from the Psalms and other passages of Scripture as you pray and worship. Let God's Word shape your prayers and expressions of worship.

Engage Your Heart: Approach prayer and worship with sincerity and openness. Pour out your heart to God, expressing your joys, concerns and desires. Allow yourself to be fully present in His presence, surrendering all to Him.

Invite the Holy Spirit: Ask the Holy Spirit to guide you and lead you into deeper intimacy with God through prayer and worship. Surrender to His leading and allow Him to minister to your heart and help you keep His commandments.

Some interpretation is needed here to avoid confusion. When Jesus speaks of "keeping" His "commandments," He isn't referring solely to the moral law of the Old Testament. Instead, He directs us to His own commandments and the principles of self-denial He exemplifies throughout the Gospels. As genuine Christians, justified by God's grace through faith, we understand that the law reveals right behaviour. Yet, our righteous standing before God is made possible by Jesus Christ's obedience to the moral law, not our religious adherence to it.

We are justified by faith apart from the moral law, but we can still reject God's grace and fail to grow into Christ's likeness. Recognizing our limitations, God, in

His wisdom, offers practical ways to deepen our intimacy with Him, not just acquire moral knowledge. Our spiritual progress may be gradual and inconsistent. Even the sincerest believers can stumble in keeping the moral law.

However, the primary virtue for Christians is perpetual purity by a saving faith (Matthew 5:48). Our faith in Christ shapes our relationship with God and empowers us to live according to His will. As we walk in faith, we grow in intimacy with God, seeking to align our lives more closely with His commandments and the example set by Jesus Christ. While various avenues exist for spiritual growth within Christian communities and activities, I firmly believe that a fervent relationship with Jesus Christ flourishes as individuals actively pursue intimacy with God through obedience to His commandments, particularly in preaching, prayer, worship and holiness.

In John 14:15-18, Jesus assures us that as we demonstrate our love for Him by obeying His commands and nurturing a close bond with Him according to His instructions, He, as the Sovereign of the spiritual realm, will personally reveal Himself to us. Through the Holy Spirit, He grants us revelation of Himself and the truth of the Gospel.

This revelation brings forth a joy and peace that surpasses human understanding and circumstances, infusing those who diligently engage in the disciplines of preaching, worship, prayer and holiness with faith. Such faith acknowledges God's ability to bestow upon His children abundant grace to fulfill His requirements and His desire for us to foster a deep personal relationship and an accurate knowledge of Him.

Participating in these spiritual disciplines facilitates genuine spiritual growth within us, allowing us to mature in our faith and experience transformational encounters with God. Through preaching, prayer, worship and holiness, we draw closer to God, aligning our hearts with His will and experiencing His presence in profound ways.

Engaging in Scripture Study and Meditation

Engaging in Scripture study and meditation is a fundamental aspect of Christian spiritual growth and intimacy with God. The Bible, as the inspired Word of God, serves as a lamp to our feet and a light to our path (Psalms 119:105), guiding us in our journey of faith and revealing God's character, will and promises.

Remember, with utmost sincerity, our steadfast commitment that each time we immerse ourselves in the sacred scriptures, we are not only inspired but also empowered to "do a good turn daily," thereby demonstrating our love for our Heavenly Father. In the pages of the Bible, we discover a divine pathway to God, disguised within one of the most magnificent displays of His love for us.

Through the scriptures, He continually reveals moral and spiritual commandments, offering profound insights into His relationship with His children of every nation, creed, and ethnicity.

This ongoing revelation of God's truth serves as the means to our spiritual awakening, a deeply personal and gradual process guided by the Holy Spirit. No one else can ascertain or determine the proximity of our relationship with God; it is a journey we must each undertake with diligence and devotion, under the gentle guidance of the Holy Spirit. Christ Himself commanded to "Search the scriptures; for in them ye think ye have eternal life: and they are they which testify of me."

Therefore, let us earnestly prepare ourselves to stand pure in the presence of our Heavenly Father, fully comprehending the depth and breadth of His commandments. In addition, we need to "Study to shew thyself approved unto God, a workman that needeth not to be ashamed, rightly dividing the word of truth" (2 Timothy 2:15). Engaging in the study and meditation of scripture becomes paramount in our spiritual journey. While prayer is vital, it is through scripture study and meditation that we most clearly discern the voice of our Father. The Holy Spirit does not simply provide easy answers or remove all doubts, but He faithfully leads us to knowledge and understanding.

As we delve into the Scriptures, doubts and uncertainties are dispelled, and we are drawn closer to God, finding solace and guidance in His eternal Word. Scripture study involves more than just reading the Bible; it requires a deliberate and focused effort to understand and apply its teachings to our lives. In 2 Timothy 3:16-17, we learn that all Scripture is God-breathed and useful for teaching, rebuking, correcting, and training in righteousness, equipping us for every good work. Therefore, studying the Bible involves not only reading but also reflecting on its meaning, context, and implications for our lives.

Meditation, on the other hand, involves contemplation and reflection on God's Word. In Joshua 1:8, God instructs Joshua to meditate on His Word Day and night, emphasizing its importance in achieving success and prosperity in life. Similarly, Psalms 1:2-3 describes the blessedness of the one who meditates on God's Law Day and night, likening them to a tree planted by streams of water, yielding fruit in season and prospering in all they do.

Engaging in Scripture study and meditation allows us to:

Know God Intimately: Through the study of Scripture, we come to know God's character, attributes, and purposes more deeply. It deepens our relationship with Him as we discover His love, faithfulness, and sovereignty.

Understand His Will: Scripture reveals God's will for our lives, guiding us in making decisions, discerning right from wrong, and living according to His principles.

Receive Guidance and Wisdom: As we meditate on God's Word, the Holy Spirit illuminates its truths to our hearts and minds, providing us with wisdom, insight, and discernment for navigating life's challenges.

Experience Transformation: Scripture study and meditation have the power to transform our hearts and minds, conforming us to the image of Christ. As we internalize God's Word, it shapes our attitudes, beliefs, and behaviours, leading to spiritual growth and maturity.

Find Strength and Encouragement: In times of trials, temptations, and uncertainties, God's Word provides us with strength, comfort, and hope. Through Scripture study and meditation, we are reminded of God's promises, His faithfulness, and His presence with us always. Therefore, engaging in Scripture study and meditation is essential for every believer seeking to grow in their relationship with God. It is a spiritual discipline that nourishes our souls, transforms our lives, and equips us to fulfill God's purposes in the world.

Cultivating a Lifestyle of Holiness and Righteousness

The essence of nurturing our relationship with God is to be like Christ in character. This is the gamut of the Christian life which distinguishes saints from religious sinners and proselytes. A clear picture of this is presented in Luke 1:74-75 which says, "That he would grant unto us, that we being delivered out of the hands of our enemies might serve him without fear; In holiness and righteousness before him, all the days of our life."

Also, a practicable illustration of this is elucidated in Titus 2:11-12 which states the major lesson of grace saying, "For the grace of God that bringeth salvation hath appeared to all men, Teaching us that, denying ungodliness and worldly lusts, we should live soberly, righteously and godly, in this present world."

Summarily, in nurturing our relationship with God, the imperatives of the foregoing are absolutely instructive as corroborated in Hebrews 12:14 which also says, "Follow peace with all men, and holiness, without which no man shall see the Lord."

CHAPTER FIVE

OVERCOMING OBSTACLES TO YOUR FIRST LOVE

"Hear, O Israel: The Lord our God is one Lord: And thou shalt love the Lord thy God with all thine heart, and with all thy soul, and with all thy might" (Deut. 6:4-5).

Overcoming obstacles to first love entails a profound journey of spiritual renewal and rekindling of one's passion for God. Just as the church in Ephesus faced challenges in maintaining their fervent devotion to Christ (Revelation 2:1-7), believers of today encounter various obstacles that hinder their intimate relationship with God. How do we overcome?

Identifying the Obstacles: The first step in overcoming obstacles to first love is recognizing and acknowledging the factors that have diminished one's passion for God. These obstacles can vary widely, from the cares and distractions of life to unresolved sin, spiritual complacency or even, external pressures and influences.

Repentance and Renewal: Once the obstacles are identified, repentance becomes essential. Repentance involves a heartfelt turning away from anything that hinders our love for God and a sincere desire to return to Him wholeheartedly. This process of repentance leads to spiritual renewal where God restores our passion for Him and revitalizes our relationship with Him.

Returning to the Source: Overcoming obstacles to first love requires a deliberate return to the source of our faith - Jesus Christ. Just as Jesus admonished the Ephesian church to "Remember therefore from whence thou art fallen, and repent, and do the first works; or else I will come unto thee quickly, and will remove thy candlestick out of his place, except thou repent." (Revelation 2:5), believers are called to revisit the foundational practices of their faith such as prayer, worship, studying God's Word, fellowship with other believers and holy lifestyle.

Cultivating Intimacy: Intimacy with God is nurtured through consistent communion with Him. This involves spending quality time in His presence, seeking His face and allowing His Spirit to work in our hearts. As we cultivate intimacy with God, our love for Him deepens and the obstacles that once hindered our relationship begin to fade away.

Perseverance and Trust: Overcoming obstacles to first love is not always easy and it requires perseverance and trust in God's faithfulness. Just as the apostle Paul exhorted the Philippians to "… press toward the mark for the prize of the high calling of God in Christ Jesus" (Philippians 3:14), believers are called to press on in their pursuit of God's love, trusting that He will empower them to overcome every obstacle.

Community and Accountability: Believers are not meant to overcome obstacles to first love alone. Community support and accountability play crucial roles in the journey of spiritual renewal. Surrounding oneself with fellow believers who can encourage, challenge and pray for one another fosters a culture of spiritual growth and renewal.

Walking in Obedience: Ultimately, overcoming obstacles to first love requires a lifestyle of obedience to God's commands. Jesus said, "If ye love me, keep my commandments." (John 14:15). As believers walk in obedience to God's Word, His love is perfected in them, and they experience the fullness of intimacy with Him.

In my experience, and according to the principles of true love outlined in the Bible, the answer is unequivocally yes. Genuine love, rooted in God's love, has the power to overcome any obstacle. Rather than merely recognizing the loss of our first love, our focus should be on actively overcoming the obstacles that lead to its decline. Throughout Scripture, stumbling blocks to faith and love are mentioned repeatedly.

Romans 14:13 and 1 Corinthians 8:9 caution us that these stumbling blocks can even come from other believers. Therefore, it is crucial for us to be sensitive to the needs of our fellow Christians and offer them our support and encouragement. Furthermore, 2 Corinthians 6:3-10 highlights how stumbling blocks can also arise from those who oppose the gospel. However, our steadfast testimony and unwavering love can serve as a powerful counter to these obstacles. Jesus Himself condemned the stumbling blocks of faith in the Gospels, urging us to maintain our testimony and continuously grow in our relationships with others.

Through our love, patience and unwavering commitment to Christ, we can effectively navigate and overcome the stumbling blocks that threaten our first love. In doing so, we not only strengthen our own faith, but also become vessels through which others can be led to experience the transformative power of God's love. In essence, overcoming obstacles to first love is a transformative journey that involves repentance, renewal, intimacy with God, perseverance, community support and obedience to God's commands. By God's grace and through the empowering work of His Spirit, believers can rediscover and rekindle their passionate love for Him, overcoming every obstacle that stands in the way.

Dealing with Distractions and Busyness

"Now it came to pass, as they went, that he entered into a certain village: and a certain woman named Martha received him into her house. And she had a sister called Mary, which also sat at Jesus' feet, and heard his word. But Martha was cumbered about much serving, and came to him, and said, Lord, dost thou not care that my sister hath left me to serve alone? bid her therefore that she help me. And Jesus answered and said unto her,

Martha, Martha, thou art careful and troubled about many things: But one thing is needful: and Mary hath chosen that good part, which shall not be taken away from her." (Luke 10:38-42). Dealing with distractions and busyness is a common challenge faced by many believers in their spiritual journey.

In today's fast-paced world filled with numerous responsibilities, demands and distractions, it can be difficult to maintain a consistent focus on God and prioritize spiritual matters. However, the Bible provides guidance and wisdom on how to overcome these obstacles and cultivate a deeper relationship with God amidst the busyness of life.

Seek First the Kingdom of God: In Matthew 6:33, Jesus teaches us to prioritize seeking God's Kingdom above all else. This means placing God at the center of our lives and making Him our highest priority, even amidst our busy schedules and daily tasks. By seeking God first in all things, we align our hearts with His will and open ourselves to His guidance and presence throughout the day.

Set Aside Time for God: Just as we allocate time for work, family and other activities, it is essential to carve out dedicated time for prayer, Bible study and worship. In Mark 1:35, we see Jesus rising early in the morning to spend time alone with the Father in prayer.

Similarly, finding a consistent time and place for spiritual disciplines can help us stay focused and connected with God amidst the distractions of life.

Guard Your Heart and Mind: Proverbs 4:23 instructs us to guard our hearts above all else, for everything we do flows from it. This involves being mindful of the influences and distractions that can pull us away from God's presence and truth. Whether it is excessive screen time, worldly entertainment or negative thoughts, we must be vigilant in protecting our hearts and minds from anything that hinders our relationship with God.

Practice Mindfulness and Presence: In Psalms 46:10, God encourages us to "be still and know that I am God." Amidst the busyness of life, it is crucial to cultivate moments of stillness and mindfulness where we can quiet our hearts and attentively listen to God's voice. By practicing the discipline of being present in the moment, we can experience God's peace and presence in the midst of chaos and distractions.

Simplify and Prioritize: Sometimes, busyness and distractions stem from over-commitment and a lack of priorities. In Luke 10:41-42, Jesus gently reminds Martha that Mary has chosen what is better by sitting at His feet and listening to His teaching. Like Mary, we must prioritize spending time with God over the busyness of life's demands. This may involve simplifying our schedules, saying no to unnecessary commitments and intentionally making room for God in our lives.

Stay Connected to the Body of Christ: Hebrews 10:24-25 encourages us to "consider how we may spur one another on toward love and good deeds, not giving up meeting together" (NIV). Regular fellowship with other believers provides accountability, encouragement and support in our spiritual journey. By staying connected to the body of Christ, we can draw strength from one another and navigate life's distractions with greater resilience and faith.

Meanwhile, the believers in Ephesus were commended by the Lord for their hard work, perseverance and endurance in serving Jesus' name. However, amidst their busy service, they had neglected the most crucial aspect: their unshakeable adoration of Christ. They had allowed distractions, even their noble cause of serving Jesus, to overshadow their first love for Him. Jesus desires our active engagement in good works, but not at the expense of our relationship with Him in holiness.

Similarly, like lovebirds absorbed in their intimate conversation, we should prioritize cultivating a deep, passionate relationship with Jesus. Just as those lovebirds seemed oblivious to the world around them, we should immerse ourselves in the presence of Christ, allowing His gaze, footsteps and voice to captivate us. This requires setting aside time for intimate communion with Him, allowing Him to lead us into deeper devotion. It is essential to recognize that distractions and busyness can hinder our spiritual passion and intimacy with Christ.

While it is commendable to be diligent in serving the Lord, we must guard against allowing our service to overshadow our relationship with Him. Jesus commended the believers in Ephesus for their hard work and endurance, but He also admonished them to remember their first love for Him. Therefore, let us strive to maintain a balance between serving the Lord faithfully and nurturing our relationship with Him. By prioritizing intimate communion with Christ, we can cultivate a deep and abiding love for Him that transcends our earthly distractions and busyness.

In conclusion, dealing with distractions and busyness requires intentional effort, discipline and reliance on God's grace. By seeking God first, setting aside time for Him, guarding our hearts and minds, practicing mindfulness, simplifying our lives and staying connected to the body of Christ, we can overcome distractions and deepen our relationship with God amidst the busyness of life.

Addressing Spiritual Dryness and Apathy

This is an active engagement in overcoming the state of spiritual stagnation, replacing "dryness and apathy" with "renewed spiritual vigour," which conveys a sense of energetic enthusiasm in one's spiritual journey. Addressing this state of spiritual dryness and apathy is a crucial aspect of the Christian journey, as it can hinder our relationship with God and diminish our spiritual vitality.

Throughout the Bible, we find examples of individuals who experienced seasons of spiritual dryness and apathy, as well as guidance on how to overcome these challenges and renew our passion for God. However, the significance of repentance cannot be overstated, as it serves as the gateway to experiencing first love. When one truly repents, it signifies a profound understanding of their sinful state and the distance it creates between them and God. It is a humble turning towards God, marked by meekness and awe and a willingness to forsake all traces of wrongdoing. However, authentic repentance goes beyond mere acknowledgment of sin; it involves building faith in God.

To nurture faith, one must immerse themselves in Scripture where God's faithfulness is vividly portrayed through the accounts of faithful individuals in the past. Through the stories of these men and women of faith, one can draw inspiration and trust in God's timing, knowing that waiting often precedes miraculous interventions. Spiritual dryness, characterized by a sense of darkness and the absence of God's presence, can lead to apathy — an indifference towards spiritual matters. This indifference signifies a loss of interest in God and a lack of spiritual passion.

Addressing spiritual dryness and apathy is essential for restoring one's first love for Christ. Without resolving these issues, the fervent desire to draw near to God diminishes and the fire of spiritual passion is extinguished. One biblical approach to addressing spiritual dryness and apathy is through self-examination and repentance. In Psalms 139:23-24, King David prays, "Search me, O God, and know my heart: try me, and know my thoughts: And see if there be any wicked way in me and lead me in the way everlasting." By honestly examining our hearts and acknowledging any areas of sin or disobedience, we open the door for God to cleanse and renew us.

Another key aspect is prayer and seeking God's presence. In Psalms 63:1-2, David writes, "O God, thou art my God; early will I seek thee: my soul thirsteth for thee, my flesh longeth for thee in a dry and thirsty land, where no water is; To see thy power and thy glory, so as I have seen thee in the sanctuary." Through earnest prayer and seeking God's presence, we can experience a refreshing and revitalizing encounter with Him.

Furthermore, engaging with Scripture and meditating on God's Word is essential for overcoming spiritual dryness and apathy. In Joshua 1:8, God instructs Joshua, "This book of the law shall not depart out of thy mouth; but thou shalt meditate therein day and night, that thou mayest observe to do according to all that is written therein: for then thou shalt make thy way prosperous, and then thou shalt have good success."

By immersing ourselves in Scripture and allowing God's Word to penetrate our hearts, we find nourishment and renewal for our souls. Additionally, fellowship with other believers and participation in worship and church activities can play a significant role in overcoming spiritual dryness and apathy. Hebrews 10:24-25 encourages us, "And let us consider one another to provoke unto love and to good works: Not forsaking the assembling of ourselves together, as the manner of some is; but exhorting one another: and so much the more, as ye see the day approaching" Through fellowship and worship, we can draw strength and encouragement from our brothers and sisters in Christ.

In practical application, it is essential to prioritize these spiritual disciplines in our daily lives. Setting aside dedicated time for prayer, Scripture reading, fellowship and worship can help us maintain a vibrant and active relationship with God. Additionally, being intentional about seeking God's presence and examining our hearts regularly can prevent spiritual dryness and apathy from taking root in our lives.

Therefore, combating spiritual dryness and apathy requires deliberate efforts to reconnect with God through prayer, Scripture reading and fellowship with other believers. It involves seeking God's presence earnestly and allowing His Word to reignite the flames of spiritual passion within our heart. Through repentance, faith-building and a renewed focus on spiritual disciplines, one can overcome spiritual dryness and apathy, leading to a restoration of their first love for Christ.

Breaking Free from Sin and Temptation

In this exploration, we delve into the biblical principles that guide believers on the path to overcoming sin and temptation. It is a journey of self-reflection, repentance and reliance on the transformative power of faith. By harnessing divine strength and wisdom, one can break the chains of sin and walk in the light of grace and redemption. This path is not merely about avoidance, but about the active pursuit of righteousness where each step forward is a testament to the soul's liberation from the shackles of worldly temptations.

Our human tendency is to believe that our good deeds can earn us salvation, but the truth, as Romans 7:7 reveals, is quite different. This verse exposes our inherent sinful nature, stating, "What shall we say then? Is the law sin? God forbid. Nay, I had not known sin, but by the law: for I had not known lust, except the law had said, thou shalt not covet." Here, the law serves as a mirror, reflecting our shortcomings and revealing the depth of our sinfulness. It highlights our propensity to covet and sin, underscoring the need for redemption. Yet, despite our sinfulness, we are not left condemned under the weight of the law. Jesus Christ, through His sacrificial death on the cross, paid the ultimate price for our sins, offering us forgiveness and reconciliation with God.

Escaping the Trap of Sin: The Bible defines sin as anything that falls short of God's perfect standard (Romans 3:23) and temptation as the lure to engage in sinful behaviour

(James 1:14). Both are inherent in the human experience due to the fallen nature of humanity (Romans 5:12). Recognize that sin and temptation are universal struggles and acknowledging them is the first step toward overcoming them. Regularly examine your heart and actions in the light of God's Word to identify areas of weakness.

Sin poses a significant obstacle to our passion for God, entangling us in its temporary allure and enslaving us to the desires of the flesh. However, the New Testament assures us that through Jesus Christ, we can find liberation from sin's bondage. Romans 6:23 declares, "For the wages of sin is death, but the gift of God is eternal life in Christ Jesus our Lord." Here, we grasp the severity of sin's consequences, but also the immeasurable gift of salvation through Christ.

Life Application: To break free from the grip of sin, we must lean on the grace extended to us through Jesus Christ's sacrifice on the cross. By acknowledging our need for His forgiveness and surrendering to His transformative power, we can overcome sin's entanglements and embrace the abundant life God offers.

Abounding Grace Over Sin: Despite the prevalence of sin, grace abounds even more abundantly. Romans 5:20-21 affirms, "The law was brought in so that the trespass might increase. But where sin increased, grace increased all the more, so that, just as sin reigned in death, so also grace might reign through righteousness to bring eternal life through Jesus Christ our Lord." Here, we witness the surpassing power of grace to conquer sin and usher in eternal life.

Life Application: Our salvation is not attained through our own efforts, but is a gracious gift bestowed upon us through faith in Jesus Christ. When we embrace this truth and place our trust in His redemptive work, sin's dominion over us is broken and we are empowered to live victoriously in the Spirit as beloved children of God.

The Power of Prayer and Scripture: Jesus Himself set an example by using Scripture to resist temptation during His time in the wilderness (Matthew 4:1-11). Additionally, He taught His disciples to pray for deliverance from temptation (Matthew 6:13). Cultivate a habit of prayer and immerse yourself in God's Word. Pray for strength and wisdom to overcome temptation and meditate on Scripture to renew your mind and fortify your spirit against sinful desires.

Accountability and Community: The New Testament emphasizes the importance of accountability within the body of believers (Galatians 6:1-2; James 5:16). Sharing struggles with trusted brothers and sisters in Christ fosters mutual support and encouragement.

Seek out accountability partners or join a small group where you can openly share your struggles and receive prayer and guidance.

Surround yourself with fellow believers who can walk alongside you in your journey towards true freedom from sin.

Fleeing Temptation and Pursuing Righteousness: Scripture instructs us to flee from temptation rather than flirt with it (1 Corinthians 10:13; 2 Timothy 2:22). Instead, we are called to actively pursue righteousness and holiness (1 Timothy 6:11). Develop strategies to avoid situations or environments that may lead to temptation. Replace sinful habits with positive, God-honouring activities. Focus your energy on serving others and growing in your relationship with God.

Embracing God's Grace and Forgiveness: While we strive for holiness, we may inevitably fall short (Romans 3:23). Yet, God's grace is abundant and His forgiveness is freely offered to those who repent and turn to Him (1 John 1:9). Understand that overcoming sin and temptation is a process and setbacks may occur. When you stumble, humbly confess your sins to God and accept His forgiveness. Allow His grace to empower you to press on in your journey toward spiritual growth.

In conclusion, breaking free from sin and temptation is both an instantaneous process and a lifelong pursuit that requires a combination of spiritual disciplines, accountability and reliance on God's grace. By integrating these biblical teachings into our lives and applying them consistently, we can experience true freedom and transformation in Christ. In other words, our deliverance from sin and the restoration of our relationship with God are made possible solely through the grace of Jesus Christ.

As we embrace this truth and live in the reality of His grace, we are liberated from sin's bondage and empowered to walk in righteousness and freedom.

CHAPTER SIX

THE BLESSINGS OF RECALLING YOUR FIRST LOVE

Drawing from the essence of biblical teachings, this theme reflects on the profound impact of rekindling the initial fervour and commitment of one experiences at the beginning of their faith journey. It is about rediscovering the purity and depth of that first encounter with divine love and allowing it to bear fruit in every aspect of life.

By remembering our first love, we are inspired to live out our faith with renewed passion, embodying the virtues of love, joy, peace and patience that are indicative of a spiritually fruitful life. Not only does Jesus offer commendation to those who faithfully endure, but He also promises a profound reward to those who overcome. In Revelation 2:7, He declares, "To him who overcomes, I will grant to eat of the tree of life, which is in the Paradise of God."

Here, "Paradise" symbolizes the glorious reign of Christ during the millennial kingdom and beyond, portraying the ultimate destination of believers in the hands of Jesus Christ. The mention of the tree of life serves as a sweet reminder of how our passion for God is reignited through our journey of faith. Life in the Spirit is indeed a partnership with Christ, a deep relationship marked by intimacy and profound communion.

A tangible fruit of this transformative journey is zealous service. Our hearts overflow with gratitude for the Lord's work in our lives, both present and future. We serve not out of obligation, but out of a fervent desire to honour Him Who has redeemed us. If you have embarked on the journey of self-examination, walking through the door of suffering, confession and seeking absolution, take heart. The fruit of this process is multifaceted. First and foremost, it results in the commendation of the Lord Himself. As Revelation 2:5-6 admonishes, remembering our initial love and returning to our first works is crucial. The Lord acknowledges our efforts, even commending us for our stand against evil.

Even, correction from the Lord, such as the removal of His lampstand from a church, bears fruit. It serves as a merciful act aimed at drawing us back to Him. Through His loving discipline, we are redirected onto the path of righteousness and restoration.

In conclusion, the journey of faith involves overcoming trials, embracing correction and passionately serving the Lord. As we persevere in our walk with Him, we can rest assured that our efforts are not in vain. Ultimately, our reward is found in the intimate fellowship with Christ and the eternal blessings awaiting us in His glorious presence.

Let us explore the biblical teaching and spiritual life application regarding "The Fruit of Remembering Your First Love."

In Revelation 2:4-5, Jesus addresses the church in Ephesus, commending them for their perseverance and endurance, but rebukes them for forsaking their first love: "But I have this against you, that you have abandoned the love you had at first. Remember therefore from where you have fallen; repent and do the works you did at first."

Rekindling Passion for God: Just as the church in Ephesus was called to remember and return to their first love for Christ, we too are encouraged to reflect on our initial fervour and passion for Him. This entails recalling the joy, zeal and intimacy we experienced when we first encountered His love. Take time to reflect on your spiritual journey and revisit moments of encountering God's love for the first time. Recall the excitement, devotion and commitment you felt. Through prayer, worship and meditating on Scripture, seek to reignite that passion and intimacy with God.

Cultivating a Heart of Devotion: Our relationship with God thrives on love, devotion and intimacy. When we prioritize our love for Him above all else, it bears fruit in every aspect of our lives. Make a conscious effort to prioritize your relationship with God above all other pursuits. Dedicate time daily for prayer, Bible study and worship. Cultivate a heart of devotion by expressing your love for Him in both words and actions.

Fostering Authentic Community: Our love for God naturally overflows into love for others. Just as the early church demonstrated fervent love and unity, we are called to foster authentic community centered on Christ's love. Engage in meaningful relationships within your church community. Be intentional about loving and serving others, sharing the love of Christ through acts of kindness, encouragement and support.

Living Out God's Love: Love is not merely a feeling, but a way of life. As followers of Christ, we are called to love God wholeheartedly and to love our neighbours as ourselves. Live out God's love in practical ways by serving others, showing compassion to the marginalized and extending forgiveness and grace to those who have wronged you. Let your love for God be evident in your words and deeds, reflecting His love to the world around you.

Bearing Fruit That Lasts: When we abide in Christ and remain rooted in His love, we bear fruit that glorifies God and blesses others. Surrender to the work of the Holy Spirit in your life, allowing Him to cultivate the fruit of love, joy, peace, patience, kindness, goodness, faithfulness, gentleness and self-control (Galatians 5:22-23). As you abide in Christ and walk in obedience to His Word, you will bear fruit that lasts for eternity.

In conclusion, remembering and returning to our first love for Christ is essential for spiritual vitality and fruitfulness. As we cultivate a heart of devotion, foster authentic community, live out God's love and bear fruit that glorifies Him, we will experience the abundant life and fulfillment that comes from abiding in His love.

A Journey to Renewed Purpose and Mission

In the light of biblical wisdom, this book explores the transformative experience of rediscovering one's divine calling. It is about aligning with the spiritual insight that illuminates our life's path, leading us to a purpose that transcends our own ambitions. This renewed sense of mission is not just a personal awakening, but a call to action, inspiring us to serve and uplift others as we fulfill our God-given destiny. It is a reminder that our true purpose is found in the pursuit of a life that reflects the love, compassion and righteousness at the heart of our faith.

If I were to merely bask in the euphoria of my spiritual encounter with God without action, it would amount to mere infatuation. Do you recall the fervour of your first love—not merely in romantic terms, but in the depth of spiritual experience? Overflowing with gratitude and energy, I sought to channel this newfound zeal into meaningful action. Even in the simplicity of obedience, I recognized the heightened joy bubbling within me.

It wasn't about grand gestures or prestigious positions; it was about surrendering to God's will and serving with a heart full of gratitude and love. In this moment, we should understand that the true fulfillment and purpose are found, not in extravagant displays of devotion, but in humble obedience and faithful service to God and others. We should embrace our roles, however seemingly insignificant and discover that every act of service offered in love is precious in God's sight.

In Matthew 28:19-20, often referred to as the Great Commission, Jesus gives His disciples a clear mission: "Go ye therefore, and teach all nations, baptizing them in the name of the Father, and of the Son, and of the Holy Ghost: Teaching them to observe all things whatsoever I have commanded you: and, lo, I am with you always, even unto the end of the world. Amen." This commission extends to all believers, calling us to proclaim the Gospel and make disciples.

Rediscovering God's Calling: Just as Jesus commissioned His disciples to fulfill a specific mission, each believer is uniquely called and equipped by God for a divine purpose (Ephesians 2:10). However, amidst the busyness of life, we may lose sight of this calling and drift from our intended path. Therefore, take time to seek God in prayer and meditation on His Word, asking Him to reveal His purpose for your life.

Reflect on your passions, talents and experiences, considering how God might be leading you to serve Him and advance His Kingdom.

Embracing Kingdom Priorities: Jesus prioritized the Kingdom of God above all else, instructing His followers to seek first the kingdom and His righteousness (Matthew 6:33). Our sense of purpose is deeply intertwined with advancing God's Kingdom agenda on earth. Evaluate your priorities and commitments in the light of God's Kingdom.

Are you investing your time, resources and energy in activities that align with His purposes? Surrender any pursuits that detract from His Kingdom and commit to wholeheartedly pursuing His agenda.

Engaging in Discipleship: The Great Commission calls us to make disciples, investing in the spiritual growth and maturity of others (2 Timothy 2:2). Discipleship involves not only sharing the Gospel, but also walking alongside others in their journey of faith.

Intentionally seek opportunities to mentor and disciple others, sharing your faith, wisdom and life experiences. Be willing to invest time and effort in nurturing spiritual growth and equipping others to fulfill their own God-given purpose.

Walking in Obedience and Faithfulness: Obedience is essential in fulfilling God's purpose for our lives. As we faithfully obey His commands and follow His leading, we experience the fulfillment of His promises and the manifestation of His purposes (John 14:15; Psalms 119:105).

Trust God's guidance and step out in faith, even when His plans may seem daunting or unclear. Commit to obedience in both small daily decisions and significant life choices, trusting that God is faithfully guiding you towards His desired outcomes.

Persevering Through Challenges: Fulfilling God's mission often involves facing obstacles and adversity. However, Scripture assures us that God equips and strengthens us to overcome every challenge (Philippians 4:13). Lean on God's strength and grace as you navigate challenges and setbacks along the journey of fulfilling your purpose. Persevere in faith, knowing that God is working all things together for your good and His glory (Romans 8:28).

In conclusion, experiencing a renewed sense of purpose and mission begins with rediscovering God's calling, embracing Kingdom priorities, engaging in discipleship, walking in obedience and faithfulness and persevering through challenges.

As we align our lives with God's purposes and actively participate in His mission, we find fulfillment, joy and eternal significance in serving Him and advancing His Kingdom on earth.

Recalling Your First Love: Insights from Revelation

In the book of Revelation, Jesus tenderly addresses the church in Ephesus, acknowledging their commendable attributes, yet highlighting a critical concern—they have forsaken their first love (Revelation 2:1-7).

Understanding "First Love:" This term encapsulates the fervent devotion and intense passion believers experience when they first encounter the transformative love of Jesus Christ. It embodies the awe, wonder and deep affection ignited by comprehending God's sacrificial love through Christ.

Importance of First Love: Our relationship with Jesus should pulsate with fervour and zeal, not merely adhering to religious routines. Losing this initial fervency can render our faith mechanical and devoid of intimacy with Christ. Jesus desires not just our service, but our hearts ablaze with love for Him.

Identifying Causes of Drifting: Various factors contribute to drifting from our first love:

Busyness in commendable activities, overshadowing intimacy with Christ.

Distractions of worldly concerns diverting our focus from Him.

Complacency stemming from worldly success, leading to spiritual stagnation.

The Call to Remember: Jesus lovingly urges the Ephesian church to reminisce about their initial love for Him. This call to remembrance isn't mere nostalgia but a catalyst for realigning hearts with God's desires. Reflecting on our initial fervour prompts repentance and sparks renewal in our relationship with Christ.

Steps to Recalling Your First Love

Reflect: Recall the moments that ignited your love for Jesus initially.

Repent: Acknowledge areas where spiritual fervour has waned or complacency has crept in.

Return: Prioritize intimacy with Christ through prayer, worship and immersion in Scripture.

Rekindle: Humbly seek the Holy Spirit's fire to reignite your passion and zeal for Christ.

Application for Today: Evaluate the state of your love for Jesus — are you fervently devoted or caught in the trap of routine? Prioritize daily communion with Him, seeking His presence and listening attentively to His voice. Let your love for God overflow into love for others, reflecting the depth of your relationship with Christ.

In conclusion, our first love for Christ isn't a fleeting emotion, but a lifelong pursuit. May we continually seek to reignite the flames of passion and devotion in our hearts, fervently pursuing intimacy with the One Who first loved us.

Reigniting Joy and Passion in Your Spiritual Walk

In the spirit of biblical teachings, this discourse delves into the journey of reigniting the joy and passion that fuels our spiritual walk. It is about tapping into the profound spiritual insight that scripture offers, guiding us back to the heart of worship and devotion. This restoration process involves a deep, introspective look at our faith, removing the barriers that have dimmed our spiritual fervour and embracing the warmth of God's love anew.

As we rekindle this inner flame, we find our steps more purposeful, our hearts more alive and our journey more vibrant, reflecting the true joy and passion that comes from a life lived in harmony with the divine. "And they that know thy name will put their trust in thee: for thou, Lord, hast not forsaken them that seek thee." - Psalms 9:10.

In Psalms 16:11, David declares, "Thou wilt shew me the path of life: in thy presence is fulness of joy; at thy right hand there are pleasures for evermore." Our journey of intimacy with Jesus is not a passive occurrence; it requires intentional effort and devotion. Just as in any healthy relationship, our walk with Christ demands continual nurture and investment.

We must consciously strive to love Him more passionately each day than we did the day before. This involves seeking Him with our whole being, recognizing that to stray from His love is to venture into darkness and trouble. Jesus prioritized love for Him above all else, admonishing the Ephesian church for their waning zeal and passion. They had drifted from their first love for Christ, a fervent devotion that compels genuine believers to hunger and thirst for more of Him.

It is a love that drives us not only to delve into His Word, but also to embody its truths in our lives. Such devotion draws the attention of the world, sparking a desire for the life-transforming power of Christ in others. Yet, if our passion for Christ has dwindled, there is hope. Despite our shortcomings, God, Who abounds in mercy, offers a way of restoration to all who are willing. Through His grace and enabling Spirit, He revives our hearts, reigniting the flame of love and devotion within us.

In Psalms 51:12, David prays for restoration, saying, "Restore to me the joy of your salvation and grant me a willing spirit, to sustain me." This verse highlights the reality that even the most devout believers may experience seasons of spiritual dryness or apathy. However, God is faithful to restore joy and passion to those who earnestly seek Him.

Returning to Your First Love: In Revelation 2:4-5, Jesus admonishes the church in Ephesus for forsaking their first love. Similarly, we may find ourselves distant from the fervent passion we once had for God. Yet, just as Jesus urges the Ephesians to remember and repent, we too can return to the intimacy and zeal of our initial encounter with Him.

Take time to reflect on your spiritual journey and recall moments of profound encounter with God. Recapture the sense of awe and wonder you experienced when you first encountered His love. Through prayer, worship and meditating on Scripture, cultivate a renewed intimacy with God.

Renewing Your Mind and Spirit: Romans 12:2 exhorts believers to be transformed by the renewing of their minds. Our spiritual vitality is closely linked to the condition of our hearts and minds. When we fill our minds with the truth of God's Word and the beauty of His promises, we experience a transformation that rekindles joy and passion. Engage in regular study of Scripture, seeking to deepen your understanding of God's character and His plan for your life. Meditate on His promises and truths, allowing them to permeate your thoughts and shape your perspective. As your mind is renewed, your spirit will be revitalized.

Rekindling the Flame of Prayer and Worship: Prayer and worship are powerful catalysts for igniting passion and joy in our spiritual journey. Psalms 16:11 declares, "Thou wilt shew me the path of life: in thy presence is fulness of joy; at thy right hand there are pleasures for evermore." Cultivate a vibrant prayer life, setting aside dedicated time each day to commune with God. Pour out your heart in worship, expressing gratitude and adoration for Who He is and what He has done. Allow His presence to fill you with joy and renew your passion for Him.

Rediscovering Your God-Given Purpose: Jeremiah 29:11 assures us that God has plans to prosper us and give us hope and a future. Rediscovering our sense of purpose and calling in God's Kingdom is key to restoring joy and passion in our spiritual journey.

Seek God's guidance and direction for your life, asking Him to reveal His purpose and calling for you. Consider your gifts, passions and experiences and look for opportunities to serve others and advance God's Kngdom. When we align our lives with God's purposes, we find fulfillment and renewed zeal for Him.

Community and Fellowship: Ecclesiastes 4:9-10 emphasizes the value of companionship and mutual encouragement in the spiritual journey. Surrounding ourselves with fellow believers who can uplift and support us is essential for restoring joy and passion. Invest in authentic Christian community, participating in small groups, Bible studies or fellowship gatherings where you can share your journey with others. Lean on your brothers and sisters in Christ for support, accountability and encouragement as you seek to renew your passion for God.

In conclusion, restoring joy and passion in your spiritual journey involves returning to your first love, renewing your mind and spirit, rekindling the flame of prayer and worship, rediscovering your God-given purpose and embracing community and fellowship.

As you actively engage in these practices and seek God with sincerity and humility, He will faithfully restore the joy of your salvation and ignite a fresh passion for Him in your heart. Hence, our relationship with Jesus demands active participation and ongoing commitment. As we seek Him wholeheartedly, trusting in His unfailing love and mercy, He restores our passion and joy, leading us on the path of life and filling our hearts with the pleasures found in His presence forevermore.

Impacting Others through Your Love for God

This is to encapsulate the profound influence of genuine love for God on those around us. Drawing from biblical teachings and spiritual life application, it emphasizes that our love for God should not be contained, but rather serve as a beacon that touches lives and inspires change. It is about demonstrating God's love through actions, words and attitudes, creating ripples of positive impact that extend beyond our immediate circles. As we live out our love for God, we become vessels of His grace, agents of His love and catalysts for spiritual transformation in our communities.

In many churches today, there is an increasing trend of drifting away from seeking divine guidance, neglecting prayer and diminishing the importance of studying the Scriptures. Instead, there is a growing conformity to worldly methods and values, aligning the Body of Christ with secular ideologies. However, we are at a pivotal moment where every believer must discern between the ways of the world and the ways of God. If we choose the path of worldly indulgence, we risk alienating ourselves from God's presence.

As Christians, we are called to bring glory to God for eternity, yet there are those among us who are spiritually adrift, abandoning the God of their salvation. It is crucial that we maintain sensitivity, love and compassion for those who are teetering on the edge or have already fallen into spiritual darkness.

Jesus taught in Matthew 5:16, "Let your light so shine before men, that they may see your good works, and glorify your Father which is in heaven." Our love for God is not meant to be kept to ourselves, but to overflow into the lives of those around us, shining as a beacon of God's love and grace.

Reflecting God's Love: 1 John 4:7-8 declares, "Beloved, let us love one another: for love is of God; and every one that loveth is born of God, and knoweth God. He that loveth not knoweth not God; for God is love." Our love for others is a reflection of the love we have received from God. Cultivate a deep, intimate relationship with God through prayer, worship and studying His Word. As you experience His love, allow it to overflow into your relationships, showing kindness, compassion, and grace to those around you.

Modelling Christ's Love: Jesus exemplified love in action throughout His ministry, showing compassion to the marginalized, forgiving sinners and sacrificing Himself for the salvation of humanity. As His followers, we are called to emulate His love in our interactions with others. Look to Jesus as the ultimate Example of love and compassion. Seek to imitate His selfless love by serving others, showing kindness and extending forgiveness. Let your life be a living testimony of Christ's transformative love.

Sharing the Gospel with Love: Mark 16:15 records Jesus' command to His disciples, "And he said unto them, Go ye into all the world, and preach the gospel to every creature." Sharing the Gospel is an expression of our love for God and our desire to see others come to know Him. Share the good news of Jesus Christ with others, not with judgment or condemnation, but with love and compassion. Build relationships with people, listen to their stories and share the hope and joy found in Christ. Pray for opportunities to share the Gospel and trust the Holy Spirit to work in their hearts.

Praying for Others: James 5:16 assures us, "Confess your faults one to another, and pray one for another, that ye may be healed. The effectual fervent prayer of a righteous man availeth much." Intercessory prayer is a powerful way to impact the lives of others, demonstrating our love and concern for their well-being. Dedicate time to pray for the needs of others, lifting them up before God with faith and compassion. Pray for their salvation, healing, provision and spiritual growth. Trust that God hears and answers prayers offered in love and faith.

Living a Life of Integrity: 1 Peter 2:12 urges believers, "Having your conversation honest among the Gentiles: that, whereas they speak against you as evildoers, they may by your good works, which they shall behold, glorify God in the day of visitation." Our actions and attitudes should reflect the love of God, drawing others to Him. Live with integrity and authenticity, allowing God's love to permeate every aspect of your life. Let your actions speak louder than words, demonstrating love, kindness and compassion to those around you. By living out your faith consistently, you can impact others and glorify God in all you do.

In conclusion, impacting others through your love for God involves reflecting His love, modelling Christ's love, sharing the Gospel with love, praying for others and living a life of integrity. As you allow God's love to flow through you, you can make a profound difference in the lives of those around you, drawing them closer to God and glorifying Him through your words and deeds.

As we navigate these critical times, let us remain steadfast in seeking divine guidance, being fervent in prayer and diligent in studying God's Word. May we be vessels of His love and compassion, extending grace to those who are lost and guiding them back into the loving embrace of our Heavenly Father. Let us never waver in our commitment to glorify God in all we do, knowing that He alone is worthy of our worship and devotion.

Epilogue

REMEMBERING OUR FIRST LOVE

In the realm of God's Kingdom, there is an age-old adage that rings true: "The good can often become the enemy of the best." This truth is evident in the lives of Christians and within the Church of the Lord Jesus Christ. Consider this: it is one of the oldest schemes of the devil himself.

Reflecting on the journey of remembering our first love brings us to a pivotal moment of introspection and renewal. It is a call to revisit the passion, fervour and devotion we once had for Christ—those initial moments when His love captivated our hearts and souls.

As we journey through life, distractions and worldly concerns often dim the flame of our love for Jesus. Yet, His love remains unwavering, burning brightly even amidst our wanderings and shortcomings. He beckons us to return, to rekindle the fire of our devotion and reignite the fervent love we once knew.

In remembering our first love, we confront the reality of our spiritual journey—the highs and lows, the moments of closeness and the seasons of distance. It is an invitation to rediscover the depth of His love and the joy of intimacy with our Saviour. As Scripture admonishes us, we are not ignorant of the enemy's tactics. Wherever God is at work, we can be certain that satan is not far behind. Described as our adversary, prowling like a roaring lion seeking someone to devour, the devil employs various strategies to thwart the work of God.

A cursory study of the New Testament reveals the multifaceted approach of the enemy. He seeks to infiltrate the church with false doctrines, sow seeds of division and discord and distract God's people from the eternal truths of Christ with earthly concerns devoid of lasting value. When confronted with resistance to sin, he may resort to persecution and trials to discourage and dishearten believers.

When these tactics fail to completely derail God's work, the enemy resorts to a more subtle tactic: diversion. This insidious strategy often masquerades behind a veneer of success. Instead of deceiving, dividing or intimidating believers, satan seeks to lull them into complacency. The fervent passion once held for Jesus is replaced with a tepid acceptance of the status quo. Satan's aim is to quench the fiery zeal for Christ and His Kingdom, replacing it with a lukewarm contentment with religious routines.

Amidst all human endeavours, there is one that holds a promise of God's unending blessing: the advancement of God's Kingdom. When we engage in sharing our faith and making disciples for Christ, God has pledged to bless our efforts, multiply them and grant us success. Despite this promise, many churches in our country have either stagnated or are in decline.

So, why does this disparity exist? It is because the enemy cunningly sows seeds of distraction, leading believers away from the singular pursuit of God's Kingdom expansion.

As stewards of the Gospel, let us remain vigilant against the enemy's schemes, steadfastly committed to advancing God's Kingdom with unwavering passion and dedication. Let us not be deceived by the allure of temporal success, but rather fix our gaze on the eternal priorities of Christ's Kingdom.

Revelation chapter 2 presents a vivid image of a church, revealing why so many churches today experience decline. It portrays not just a church, but individual Christians who have allowed what is good to replace what is best in their spiritual lives.

Let us be clear: this is not a fate that has befallen our church; God is present and active among us. Yet, we must remain vigilant. We must collectively and individually guard against losing our passion. We must be on guard against becoming like the church at Ephesus. This is why the text has been preserved in God's Word — it is prophetic, preventative and prescriptive. God does not desire for us to follow in the footsteps of Ephesus.

With this in mind, we wrap our discussion summarily.

Commendation and Warning from Christ

The city of Ephesus stood as a formidable force, a hub of trade and tourism. Despite its wealth, it was steeped in paganism, housing the grand temple of Artemis. Acts 20 provides context for this church, revealing Paul's extensive ministry among them. Additionally, the book of Ephesians showcases their profound understanding of Christian doctrine and spiritual warfare.

The Ephesian church faced persecution during a tumultuous period in Christian history, yet they remained steadfast. Christ commends their diligence and doctrinal fidelity. They were not idle; their calendar brimmed with activities for the Lord. They stood firm against heresy, grounded in the Word and resilient in persecution. Outwardly, they appeared exemplary.

For these commendable traits, Christ praises them. However, a crucial insight emerges — mere works do not suffice. Christ desires heartfelt transformation. Hence, after commending them, Christ counsels them. Counsel from Christ admonishes them to return to their first love, to rekindle their passion for Him. Though they started strong, over time, their fervour waned. Despite doctrinal fidelity and endurance, they had lost their zeal. Their initial fervent love for Christ gave way to mechanical religiosity.

What occurs when we lose our first love? Legalism, self-righteousness or mechanical religiosity may replace the fervent love that once stirred our hearts. The passion that once motivated us wanes and our service becomes ritualistic. Therefore, Christ's counsel is clear: return to your first love. Keep Jesus central in your affections. Let your service be fueled by passion rather than mere obligation.

Overall, let us heed Christ's counsel to the church at Ephesus. May we guard against complacency and ritualistic religiosity, prioritizing heartfelt devotion to Christ above all else by:

Focusing on the Substance of Faith. Often, we find ourselves fixating more on the outward appearance rather than the essence of our faith. We prioritize knowledge over holiness, believing that mere accumulation of information equates to spiritual growth. Yet, true holiness is not attained through intellectual pursuits, but through an intimate relationship with God.

Pursuing Holiness Over Knowledge. The quest for personal holiness takes precedence over the pursuit of knowledge. While knowledge has its place, it should never supersede the importance of God's presence and lordship in our lives. Our focus should be on becoming more like Christ, not merely accumulating facts. As the apostle Paul reminds us in Philippians 3:8, "I count everything as loss because of the surpassing worth of knowing Christ Jesus my Lord." – NIV.

Embracing Awe and Reverence. Instead of becoming complacent in our familiarity with the Holy, we should maintain a sense of awe and reverence. Just as Isaiah trembled in the presence of God (Isaiah 6:5), we should approach Him with humility and reverence. Our reverence for God should prevent us from treating His holiness casually as the sons of Samuel did (1 Samuel 2:12).

Rekindling Evangelistic Zeal

Our love for Christ should fuel our passion for sharing the Gospel with the lost. When we lose sight of our mission to reach the world with the love of Christ, we become inwardly focused, more concerned with preserving traditions than with advancing God's Kingdom. Our churches should be fervently engaged in reaching the lost, not merely maintaining a comfortable status quo, through:

Sensitivity to the Holy Spirit. A vibrant relationship with Christ keeps us sensitive to the leading of the Holy Spirit. We are quick to repent of sins and seek reconciliation with others. Conversely, when our love for Christ wanes, we become desensitized to sin and allow discord to fester within the body of Christ.

Striving for Christlikeness. Our ultimate goal should be to become more like Christ in every aspect of our lives. Instead of comparing ourselves to others, we should measure ourselves against the perfect standard of Christ. This pursuit of Christlikeness guards against self-righteousness and fosters humility.

Putting Christ as the Center of Our Lives. **Nothing should occupy the throne of our hearts except for Christ Himself. While we may profess Christ as Lord, our actions reveal where our true allegiance lies. Success, power, pride or pleasure should never usurp Christ's rightful place in our lives.**

Maintaining Passionate Devotion. **Our relationship with Christ should be characterized by fervent love and devotion, akin to that of Stephen and Paul. Such fervour compels us to endure hardships and even lay down our lives for the sake of the Gospel.**

May we never settle for a formal, ritualistic faith, but continually pursue a vibrant, intimate relationship with our Saviour, Jesus Christ. In essence, our focus should always remain on cultivating a deep, intimate relationship with Christ, allowing His love to transform us from the inside out.

Embracing a Passionate Love for Christ. Consider the contrast between the vibrant relationship Christ desires and the lukewarm devotion many Christians exhibit today. Instead of prioritizing time with Him daily, they prioritize personal desires over His concerns. Unwilling to surrender all they are and possess to Jesus, they cling to material comforts and fear being labelled fanatical.

Surrendering All to Christ. Christ calls us to surrender everything to Him — not just part of our lives, but every aspect. He doesn't seek a mere place in our hearts; He desires complete rulership.

Our relationship with Him shouldn't be one among many passions, but the central focus of our lives.

A Call to Intimacy. Jesus longs for us to reciprocate His deep love. He demonstrated this love on the cross, willingly bearing our sins out of His boundless love for humanity. His passion for us remains as intense as ever, even amidst our failings.

Returning to Our First Love. Jesus beckons us to return to the fervent love we once had for Him. He urges us to recall the moment when we first encountered His love and grace, when nothing else mattered, but Him. He invites us to rekindle that passion and devotion.

Heeding the Divine Counsel. Failure to heed His counsel carries consequences. Christ warns that without repentance, His Spirit's fire will depart from our midst. External trappings may remain, but the power of God will be absent. A church devoid of His presence is a tragic sight indeed.

The church's passion reflects its members. The collective passion of a church mirrors that of its members. If individuals are fervent for Christ, it will manifest in the church's vitality. Conversely, lukewarmness among individuals results in a lackluster fellowship.

Personal Reflection and Response

Ultimately, this message speaks to each individual. God calls us to remember where we once stood, to return to our first love. He invites us to reignite the passion and zeal we once had for Him.

Conclusion

God's message resonates with us individually. He calls us to remember and return to our first love for Him. Let us heed His call, recalling the fervour and devotion of our initial encounter with Christ. As we do, may our love for Him burn brightly once more. In essence, the focus shifts towards personal reflection, repentance and a return to the fervent love and devotion we once had for Christ.

Akinbowale Isaac Adewumi
akindewum@gmail.com

Other Books Written By the Same Author

1. Satanic Attacks and the Way Out.
2. Victorious Christian Living Essentials.
3. Prevailing Prayers of Intercession and Supplication Guides.
4. Satanic Attacks and the Way Out (Second Edition).
5. Principles of Christian Marriage and Family Life.
6. Evangelization and Christian Development.
7. Winning the Invisible War with Christ.
8. Called to be a Soldier.
9. End Time Events.
10. Christ-Centered Parenting.
11. Prepare to Meet Your Lord.
12. Weeds Among the Wheat.
13. Church in the House.
14. Religion or Righteousness.
15. Divine Healing and Health.
16. Power of Praise and Worship.
17. And the Yoke Shall be Destroyed.
18. Discovering your God-given Potentials.
19. Our God: A Consuming Fire.
20. Call to Salvation.

Bibliography

https://digitalcommons.pepperdine.edu

https://iblp.org/how-can-return-my-first-love-lord/

https://www.christianlearning.com/Bible

https://www.desiringgod.org/articles

https://www.franklingraham.com

https://www.lifeway.com/en/articles/sermon-remember-first-love-ephesians-revelation-2

https://ifaqtheology.com

https://research.manchester.ac.uk/en/publications/framing-the-commnity-data-system-interface

www.ingramcontent.com/pod-product-compliance
Lightning Source LLC
Chambersburg PA
CBHW060400050426
42449CB00009B/1832